AF278836

HOW NOT TO STRESS-OUT

LESLEY MEYER

© **Lesley Meyer December 2019**

Photos by: Lesley Meyer

Design & Layout: Lesley Meyer

ISBN 978-0-9947216-7-9

EBook ISBN 978-0-620-76394-3

Contents

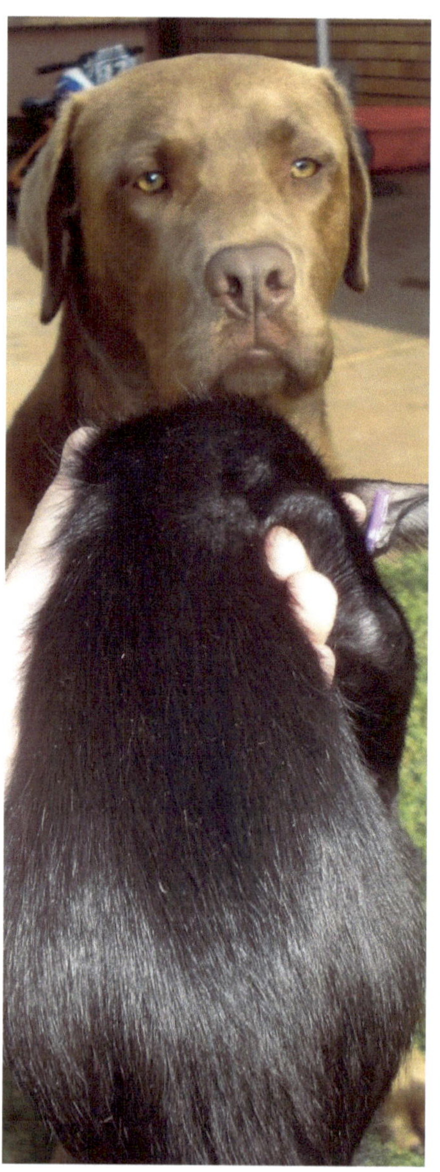

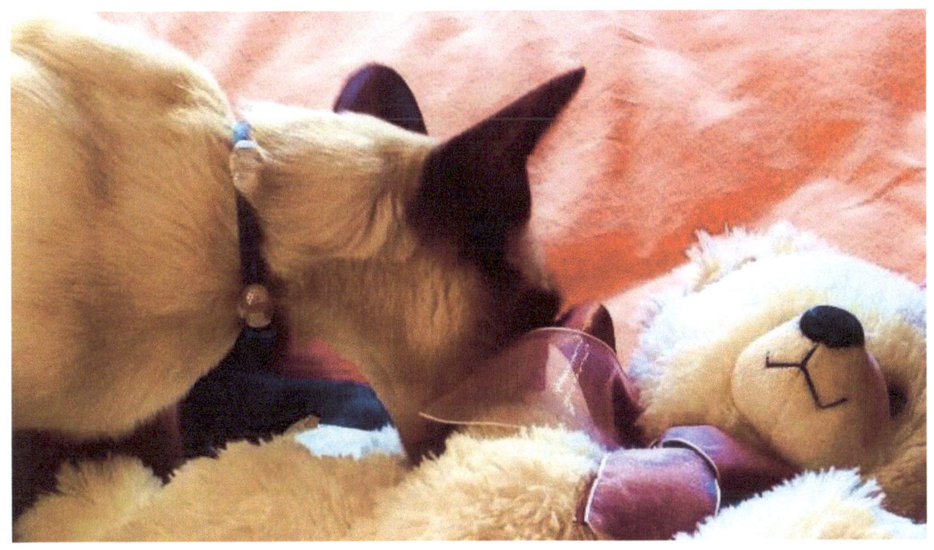

THE REALITY OF STRESS

Before I can tell you how not to stress I need to tell you how stress is created. There are three types of stress:

1. Physical stress: Where you hurt the body through lack of food, sleep, water, exercise, posture, and an injury.
2. Emotional stress: Where you experience a severe emotional trauma such as a death of a loved person or animal.
3. Mental stress: How you continuously think about your life or situations that you have experienced, be they physical or emotional.

Our body is designed to handle stress in a very special way. We see this clearly in the wild where the lion will chase the buck but when it does not succeed in catching it and walks away, the buck will lie down on the grass and shake to release the stress of the chase. Once the shaking is done the buck will get up and eat grass as if nothing has happened. It does not carry the stress of the chase into the future causing other physical problems.

As humans, we too have this mechanism built into our bodies. I have experienced it several times. My jaw and whole body shiver like when I am cold but I know I am not cold as my body temperature is warm and thus it is a stress release shiver.

If we do not allow the shiver to take place, we will store the trauma of the event somewhere in our bodies. This may create pain such as headaches, ulcers, body pain, fatigue and anxiety. If left unattended it may then escalate into panic attacks, depression or chronic pain. These symptoms may not respond to conventional treatment as it is not necessarily the right treatment. When the right treatment is given, the symptoms will clear up quickly and you can be pain-free to live a happy, stress-free life.

PHYSICAL STRESS

Our bodies are not designed to sit behind a desk all day and work on a computer. It is very important to make sure you have a form of exercise to help keep you fit and release endorphins inside your body that keep you happy and help you cope with stress. If we do have to sit for long periods of time, it is vital to get up every two hours and stretch out the body. It is also vital that you make sure your ergonomics (the set-up of your workstation to ensure correct posture) is correct for all tasks.

If the ergonomics is not correct it will put a strain on your body causing muscle spasms which then refer pain in specific areas. This poor posture you sit or stand in regularly will cause your body to grow into this posture, resulting in shortened muscles and pain. This then prevents you from assuming a normal, upright, healthy posture.

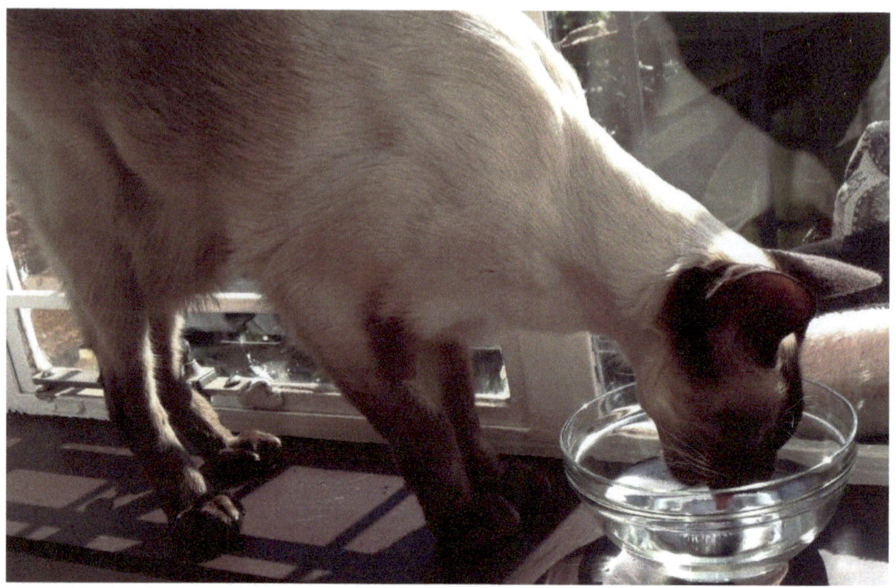

This puts strain on your joints and may cause abnormal development of your body. These muscle spasms can continue forever unless you take measures to release them. These being: stretches, exercises, massage therapy, Dry needling, relaxation/meditation, eating healthily, sleeping eight hours a night, drinking enough water, and correct posture at all times.

Physical stress is thus caused by our day-to-day routine and poor postures we maintain. It is also caused by a severe physical trauma to the body. This can be a car accident where you get a whiplash or break a body part. It can be from twisting your ankle. Any injury that you sustain to your body can result in ongoing pain if you do not treat it properly and resolve it totally. This injury, if unmanaged can continue into your adult life and may spread throughout the body causing global chronic pain. Just because you are young, does not mean that your injuries   are   not   serious!

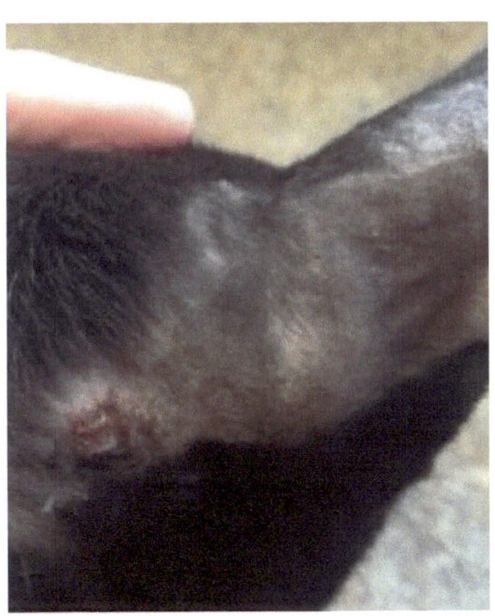
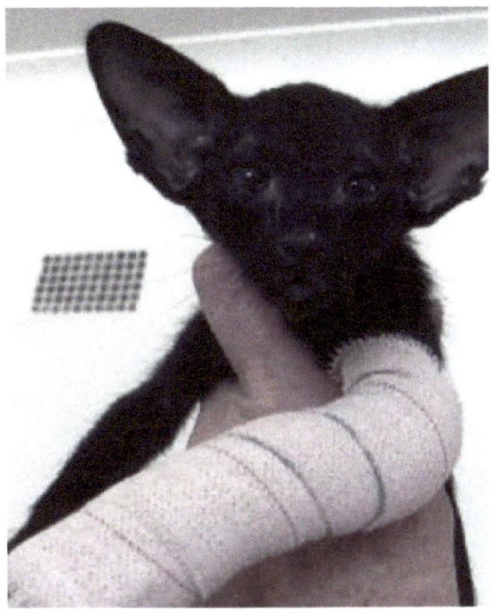

EMOTIONAL STRESS

There are obvious emotional triggers and then there are the subtle emotional triggers. The obvious ones are things like losing a family member or beloved pet, being bullied daily at school, failing a test, a break-up or having your parents get divorced.

The not so obvious ones are when people you love, talk to you in a negative way regularly. When you are constantly being told by a person you trust that you are fat or not good enough. When you are coerced, by someone you trust, into doing something you don't want to do or feel guilty about doing. Also when people talk behind your back or when they say nasty things about you on social media or when you are told to keep a secret because if you tell you will get into serious trouble.

Pressure you place on yourself to perform and get top results is emotionally exhausting. This is often done to get recognized and praised by your loved ones. You need to think about what is emotionally stressing you out, why you are doing what you are doing and then if you are not able to change the way you think about the situation to a positive viewpoint, discuss it with someone to help you see the silver lining. Try to look for the positive in all negative events.

Don't lock yourself away or avoid people to avoid being hurt. Don't stop eating because they tease you about your food. Don't avoid doing sport because you are not as good as the others.

Stand up for yourself. To those who tease you tell them **"Stop, I don't like that!"** take back your power. To those who constantly tell you that you are fat or not good enough, either tell them to **"STOP! We don't talk to each other that way! "** or ask yourself if they really have a degree in that topic to enable them to tell you from an educated position that you are stupid, fat or not good enough, or is it their own short-comings they are expressing onto you?

If they have told you to keep a secret and coerced you into doing something you feel guilty about, then go and tell someone you can trust to help you resolve the matter. You will not get into trouble, they are probably telling you this because they know that what they are doing it wrong.

MENTAL STRESS

We are all born to express love and be loving. We are addicted to love and attention. But as we grow older, our life experiences, the way our parents and influential others treat us, mould us into the people we become. We trust people less if we have been treated badly. We can change from being good, happy people to someone who has a low self-esteem and acts out just to get attention, even if it is negative attention. When the people we love and know constantly tell us that we are stupid, ugly, too fat, too thin, laugh funny, can't sing, smell or are not wanted, we will believe them.

We imprint these words into our brain. These beliefs will then be constantly validated by our life experiences as we are tuned in to see the negative side of the story, instead of the positive. Over the years these beliefs we have, change our reality and can prevent us from achieving our true potential.[1]

Many of these beliefs are not true and if you take the time to think about your experiences, learn from the experience, and thus change the way you think about it, you can succeed in life. [2–4] It is a mental choice to change the way you think. Wake up each morning and choose to be positive.

If you experience an emotional trauma, many will replay this event over and over infinitely. Making the short period of time take over your life and turn it into a difficult, depressed and unwanted life. Many of the life events one experiences are there to teach us certain lessons and mould us into the people we need to become to achieve our life purpose on Earth. These lessons are never learned from easy, fun times. They are usually taught in the most difficult of circumstances.

I was in a serious accident many years ago. I broke many bones in my body and have experienced severe pain since. I could have chosen to see this event as the worst event in my life and become depressed about it. I chose instead to see it as the most important event in my life. It lead me down the path of understanding how others in pain feel and thus I am able to empathize and treat them properly. You cannot understand unless you have experienced the same feelings.

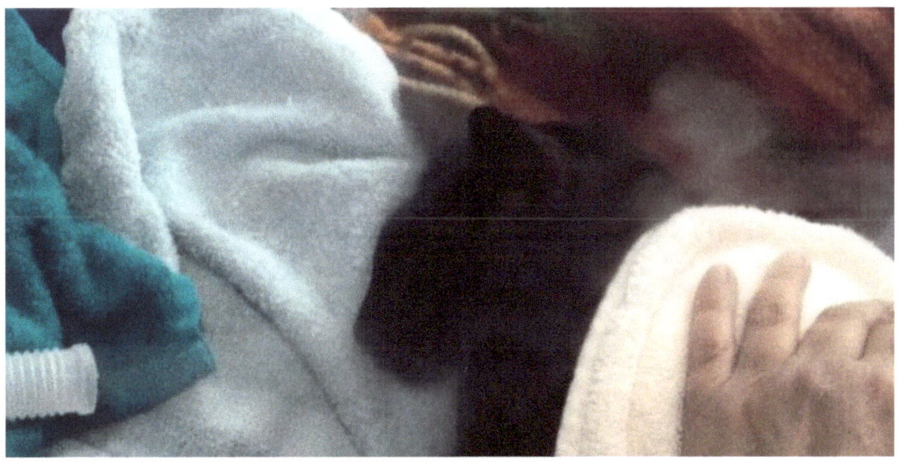

CHANGING THOUGHTS ABOUT THE TRAUMA

There are many ways to change the way you think about the events you have had the misfortune of going through. One of the techniques that I have found most useful is EFT (Emotional freedom technique) created by Dr Roger Callahan.

During this technique, you think about an event that has been traumatic for you. It can be anything. You will give it a feeling, as you must think about how it made you feel and not just rattle off the event. Once you have the feeling, you can rate this feeling on a scale of 0-10, zero being no problem and ten being a severe emotion. While thinking about this feeling and why you felt this feeling linked with the experience, you tap on the side of the hand and over face points. By thinking about the experience in a different light, you can alter the way you feel. If it was so horrendous that there is no changing the thought, you would then think up solutions to the picture. You may, for example, think of an Angel coming to your rescue and protecting you, or a white light surrounding you blocking out the image. There is no right or wrong, whatever feels good for you is right. You may even confront the person and sit them down and talk to them expressing all the feelings you had and what they have done to you, in your mind.

The brain cannot tell the difference between reality and fantasy. This is why you wake with your heart pounding and sweaty all over when you have a nightmare. This is the same with changing the memory. The brain will believe it has remembered the memory incorrectly and the new image you have imprinted on the brain will become your reality. Thus the body will release new chemicals in the body and you will feel lighter and more at peace.

Basic EFT Technique

Step 1: Choose a problem to work with

Step 2: Rate your anxiety or discomfort (where 0=no distress and 10=highest level of discomfort) when you think about it right now. (How anxious are you? How uncomfortable do you feel?) Also, close your eyes, check in your body and feel where you feel it in your body.

Step 3: Tap the karate-chop point (on the fleshy side of the hand) while you say the problem and then finish by saying that you're still ok: *Even though I have this [problem], I deeply and completely love and accept myself.* Repeat 3 times.

Step 4: Tap on each of the following stress-relief points while repeating a short reminder of the problem (for instance "this fear in my stomach")

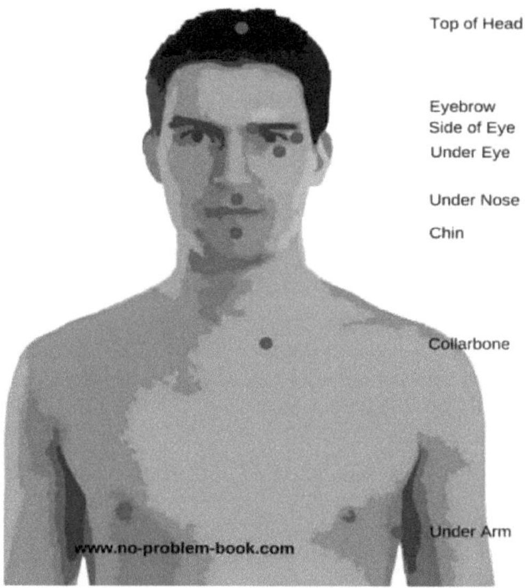

Step 5: Rate your anxiety or discomfort again. If any discomfort remains, repeat the steps above until you're down to a 0. You can adapt the Set-Up Statement (Step 3) to "Even though I still have some fear of...."

Step 6: If you're not making headway, there is a variety of trouble shooting options. Please contact me for assistance.

Liesel Teversham   www.no-problem-book.com   liesel@no-problem-book.com

EXPECTANCY MINDSET

Expectations are part of our daily lives. It is how we think and choose to live our lives. Due to the mind-body connection, expectancy produces real, neurophysiological outcomes in the body. [4] If we believe that our daily activities will help us with weight loss, then our body will accommodate and we will get the resultant weight loss.

In the book and DVD the "Secret", they talk about a dream-board and having an abundance mindset. When we focus on positive things and set up a dream-board where we allow ourselves to dream big, our subconscious will look for the opportunities to get what we have set our hearts on. We will start attracting the dreams we have put on the dream-board. This causes improved expectancy feelings.

If we do not take the time to dream big and write down our dreams and goals (bucket list), then our subconscious does not know what to focus on. Thus, if we are depressed, we should focus on finding peace and joy through EFT and pictures that depict happiness for us. People who are lucky are not "Lucky!" they have chosen to wake up every day with a positive mindset and are attracting more positivity to them. They have created their own luck through hard work and positivity. If you are unlucky, it is the same principle.

TENSION AND TRAUMA RELEASE EXERCISES (TRE)

Day-to-day living has become very stressful in the average home. This is because traffic is heavy, travelling times are long, work is full of pressures and time is scarce. There is little communication between family members. We go through life often feeling unloved, unvalued, and that we do not fit in. We are constantly being chased by the proverbial lion. Yet at the end of the day when we are ready to go to bed, we are unable to switch off the brain and relax as we still feel like the lion is chasing us. We have not allowed the body to shiver to release the stress, we are still in flight and fight mode and this puts undue stress on the body.

One can train the body to go into a shiver, releasing the tension and stress in the body. This technique is known as TRE, created by Dr David Berceli, who has written numerous books on it. There are a few exercises you go through to get the body to activate a shiver. If you have very tight muscles you may find it difficult to get the shiver fully activated. The exercises need to be done very slowly to calm the body down. When you start shivering, you can stop it at any time by straightening the legs. If this does not work, you can get someone to apply pressure onto your legs and arms.

BASIC TRE TECHNIQUE

1. Stand with your feet shoulder width apart. Rock slowly from side-to-side to the edges of your feet while breathing deeply. Rock three times to each side.

2. Place the top of your right foot on the heel of the left. As you breathe in you lift up onto your left foot. Lower yourself while exhaling. Do three on each side.

3. Place your hands on the floor. Lift the right leg slightly off the floor, inhale and exhale deeply. Repeat three times alternating your feet.

4. Stand with your feet wide apart and place your hands on the floor. Breathe in for three breaths. Stretch your arms as far to the right as you can for three deep breaths. Repeat to the left. Then place your hands between your legs stretching backwards while breathing.

5. Making fists with your hands push down on your hips and look over the right shoulder and then left while breathing slowly. Repeat three times.

6. Lean against a wall with your knees squatting at 90 degrees. Inhale and exhale three times deeply. Hang forward with your legs at shoulder width and repeat the three breaths.

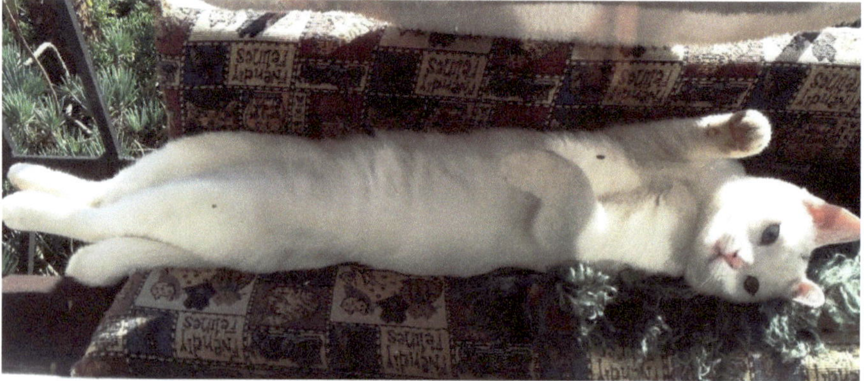

7. Lie on your back with the soles of your feet touching each other. Lift up your bottom and hold for three breaths. Lower your hips and slowly bring the knees towards each other keeping your feet together. You will start feeling a tremor deep in your body. Allow it to shake for 30-40 minutes. If you feel it is too intense then straighten your legs to stop the tremor or turn onto your side into the foetal position. Keep this position until you feel settled.

You can shake throughout the body or it can be a gentle tremor. Don't be alarmed it is normal. If you are nervous then look up a therapist who is trained in this technique.

PHYSICAL CARE

When we have had a physical trauma, it is important to ensure that the tight and painful muscles are treated and helped back to a normal, healthy, pliable state. If this is not done and you continue to exercise on the injured limb, you can cause more damage. If you are getting treatment, then exercise is good to continue with as a means of determining if the area has reached it's normal state yet. Some areas never heal after a severe injury and ongoing care will need to be taken to keep the area soft and pliable so that it does not spread to other parts of the body.

Stretching and different forms of exercise are critical for a healthy body and mind. When we exercise we release happy hormones called endorphins. These hormones help improve our expectancy state of mind and help us be more positive people so that we can increase our good luck. It is possible to over-exercise at which point it will be more catabolic than anabolic. In other words, it will break the body down more than build it up. Here your body may then get stress-fractures and other muscle injuries that can take a long time to heal.

Other ways to reduce your physical stress is to meditate or do fun things with friends, having an outlet for frustrations.

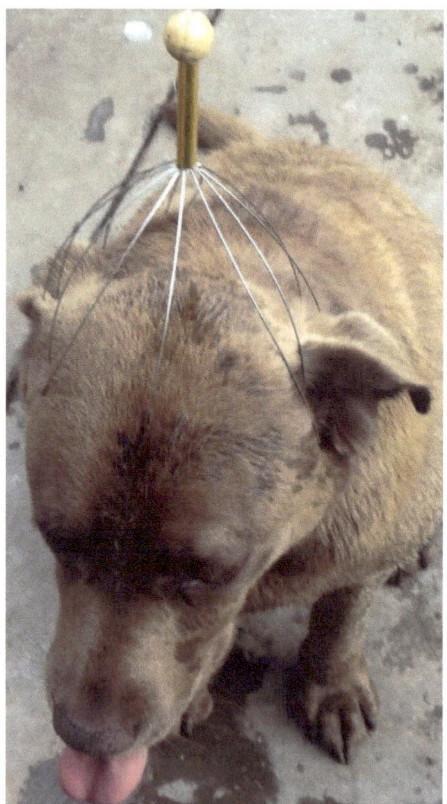

MINDFUL-THINKING

Mindful-thinking is being in the moment. In our rushed lives we often do not take note of the things around us. We do not notice the pretty spring flowers until we smell them. We do not notice our friends are unhappy until something drastic happens. We don't notice how what we say is affecting someone, we just think it's funny because others are laughing and we are craving the attention ourselves.

Mindful-thinking is taking note of the people and things around you. Taking time to think about how you should and should not behave. Taking time to do the things you need to do to keep your mind and body in a happy, healthy state as well as those around you.

It does not help to stress-out about the test that is happening next week or the project that is due. If you work diligently and stay in the moment, keeping up to date with your work and studies, then you will know the work and do well. If you expect to do well, you will study harder and prove yourself right. If you believe you are going to fail, you will worry about failing and not bother studying, proving yourself right once again.

Stay in the moment every day doing what needs to be done in time. Don't leave for tomorrow what you can do today.

 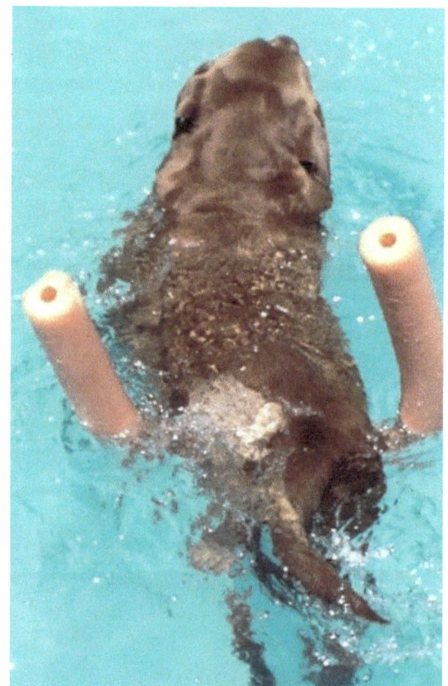

HELP ME COPE ACTIVITIES

1. Are you feeling stressed or anxious at the moment?
2. Are you physically, emotionally or mentally stressed?
3. What is causing your stress?
4. Use the EFT technique either by yourself or with a trusted friend or family member and see if you can reduce your stress levels, aim for 0.
5. Do you have an expectancy mindset or a closed, negative mindset?
6. Actively do the TRE release technique and see if you can activate a shiver.
7. Do you need any treatment to help improve any physical injuries? Who do you need to see?
8. Write a paragraph on what you perceive Mindful-thinking to be. Do you observe it in your daily life?
9. Write a paragraph on what you can do to be more positive and attract more luck to you.

REFERENCES

1. 1. Image: Maslow's Hierarchy of Needs | Simply Psychology.

2. 2. Del Sesto D. Shift Your Thinking: 200 Ways to Improve Your Life. Grand Rapids: Revell; 2016

3. 3. The greatness in you: how unleashing your infinite potential unlocks infinite possibilities for you. Wansbeck: Reach; 2016.

4. 4. Leaf C. The perfect you: a blueprint for identity. Grand Rapids, Michigan: Baker Books; 2017. 316p.

ABOUT THE AUTHOR

Lesley is a Physiotherapist with a special interest in chronic pain. She has studied extensively in a variety of different therapies to enable her to treat her patients holistically. Many of her chronic pain patients went through terrible experiences and she had to learn through EFT how to help them cope with these situations. She has read extensively on self-development and through these books has broadened her knowledge. This information has been crucial in the EFT and Matrix re-imprinting techniques she uses daily with her patients.

From the same author:
Tired of being tired to the point of being gatvol
Knights of the 21st century
Goal setting to improve your potential and self-image
Animals can be bullies too
Caring for your animals. All creatures great and small
The old "Finishing School"

Bphyst/APPI/EFT/DDN/IMS/OMT/NLC
With a special interest in chronic pain

1004 Rabie Road,
Eldoraigne X1,
Centurion
0157
South Africa
0825510388
Cope.sa@vodamail.co.za

www.ingramcontent.com/pod-product-compliance
Lightning Source LLC
Chambersburg PA
CBHW041233050726
47599CB00007B/935